W9-AGU-658

ed emberley's

PICTURE PIE

a circle drawing book

Little, Brown and Company

Boston   New York   London

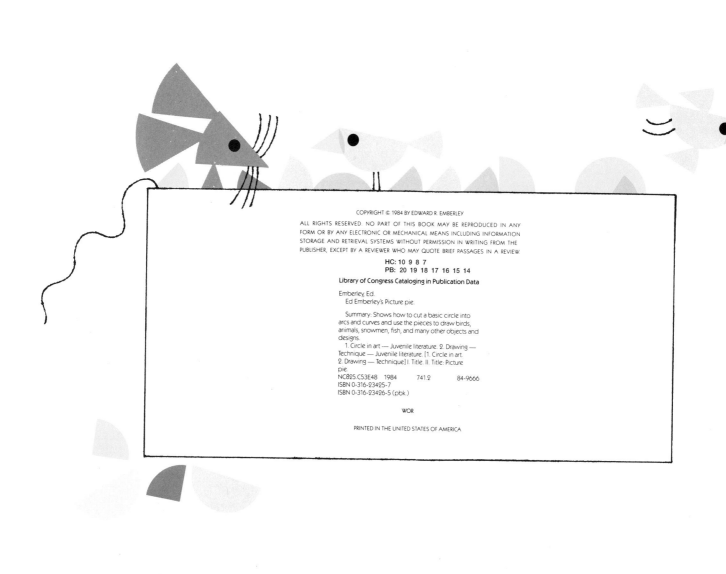

HC: 10 9 8 7
PB: 20 19 18 17 16 15 14

Library of Congress Cataloging in Publication Data

Emberley, Ed.
   Ed Emberley's Picture pie.

   Summary: Shows how to cut a basic circle into
arcs and curves and use the pieces to draw birds,
animals, snowmen, fish, and many other objects and
designs.
   1. Circle in art — Juvenile literature. 2. Drawing —
Technique — Juvenile literature. [1. Circle in art.
2. Drawing — Technique] I. Title. II. Title: Picture
pie.
NC825.C53E48   1984   741.2   84-9666
ISBN 0-316-23425-7
ISBN 0-316-23426-5 (pbk.)

WOR

PRINTED IN THE UNITED STATES OF AMERICA

This book shows how a circle

divided like a pie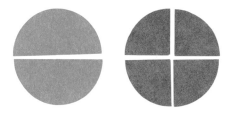

can be used to make pictures of all kinds of things

These 4 simple, basic shapes

can be put back together to make: a set of other,

more complex shapes,

(There are lots more shapes in the back of the book.)

hundreds of different designs,

(The dots : show the number and color of circles used.)

frames, borders,

and other repeat patterns,

as well as a number of birds and other things.

Here's how:

(More instruction in the back of the book.)

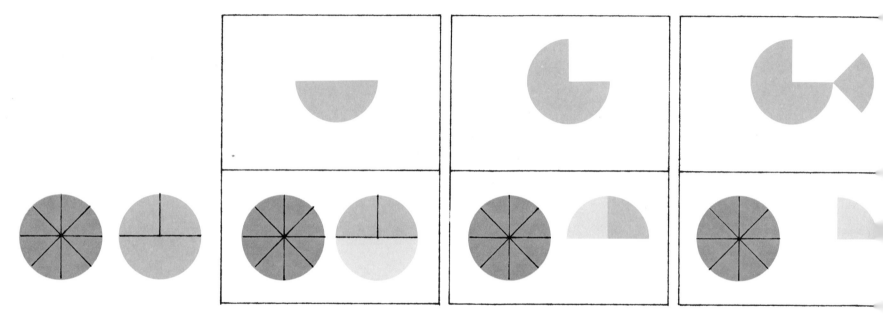

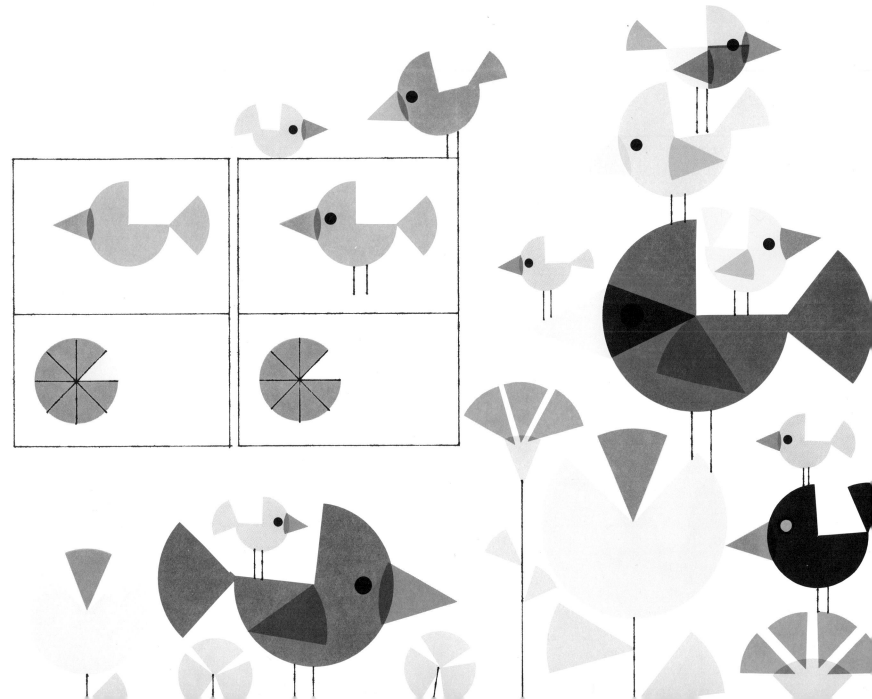

The picture pie pictures in this book can be:

1. recreated, just for the fun of it, as sort of a game or puzzle

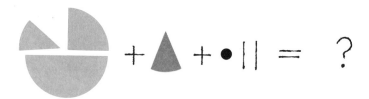 $+ \triangle + \bullet \, || \; = \; ?$

2. used "as is" for work of your own

in cut paper for signs, posters, etc.,

JUNE

	1	2	3	4	5	6
7	8	9	10	11	12	13
14	15	16	17	18	19	20
21	22	23	24	25	26	27
28	29	30				

A SPECIAL INVITATION

BULLETIN BOARD

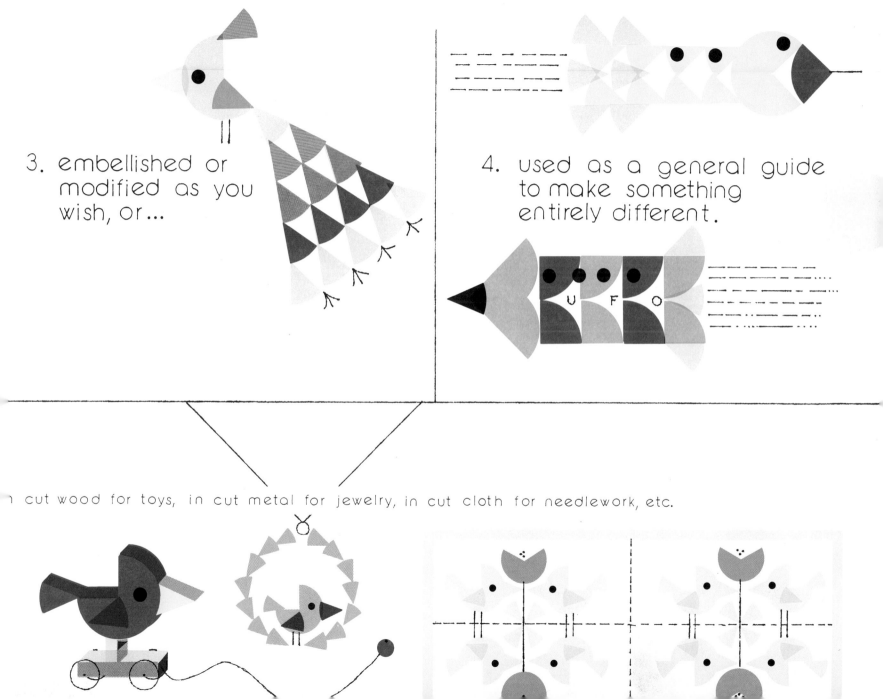

3. embellished or modified as you wish, or...

4. used as a general guide to make something entirely different.

cut wood for toys, in cut metal for jewelry, in cut cloth for needlework, etc.

A few hints for making something "entirely different." You can add:

other materials,

A lot of variety can be added by using patterned materials.

other divisions,

More variety, more possibilities.

16   32   more of the same

random divisions

other circles,

By adding circles of different sizes, it is possible to make hundreds of people, animals, and other things.

other shapes.

By adding one other shape, the square, it is possible to make thousands of people, animals, and other things.

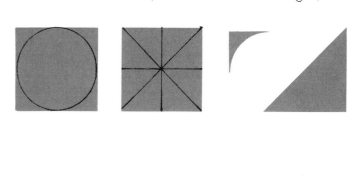

It is possible to show only a
few of the many things
that can be made
using picture pie parts;
much has been left for
you to explore, discover,
and take pleasure in.

To the back of the book.

To get started making picture pie pictures, you will need 5 things:

1. colored paper

2. something to cut it with

3. something to stick it down with

4. something to make dots and lines with

5. something to make circles with.
(You can use a compass or you can draw around a cup a can, or some other round object.)

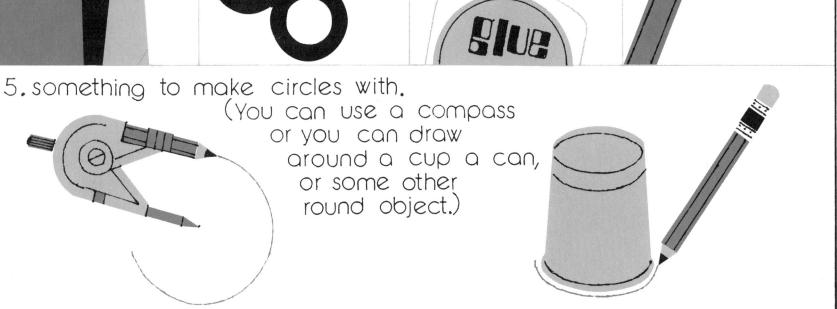

You will also have to know how to
make these 4 basic picture pie shapes.

1. start	2. fold in half	3. crease	4. unfold	5. cut along crease

All the pictures in the first part of this book were made using these 4 basic shapes.

You will be able to figure out how to make many just by looking at them.

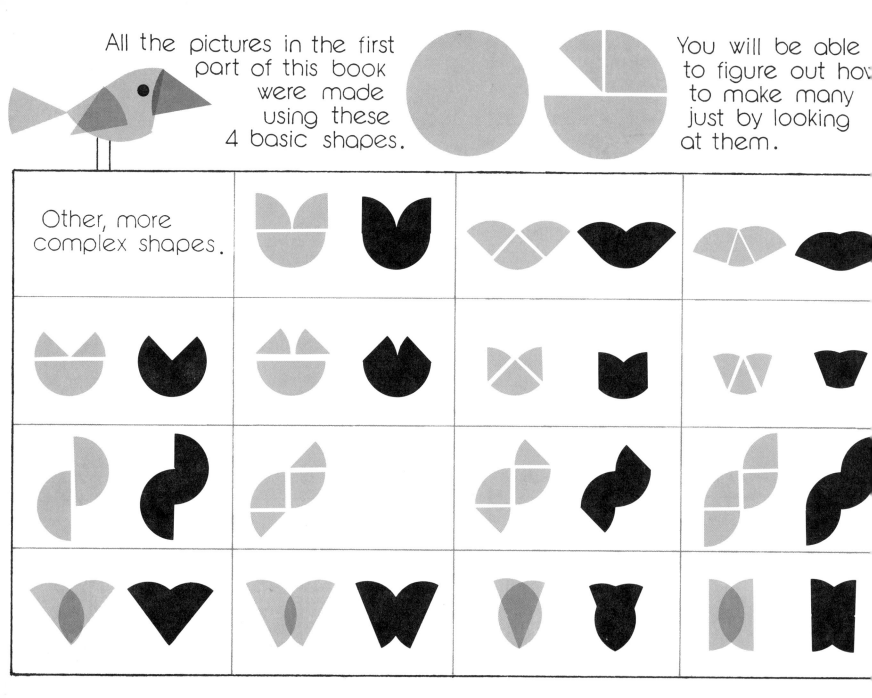

Other, more complex shapes.

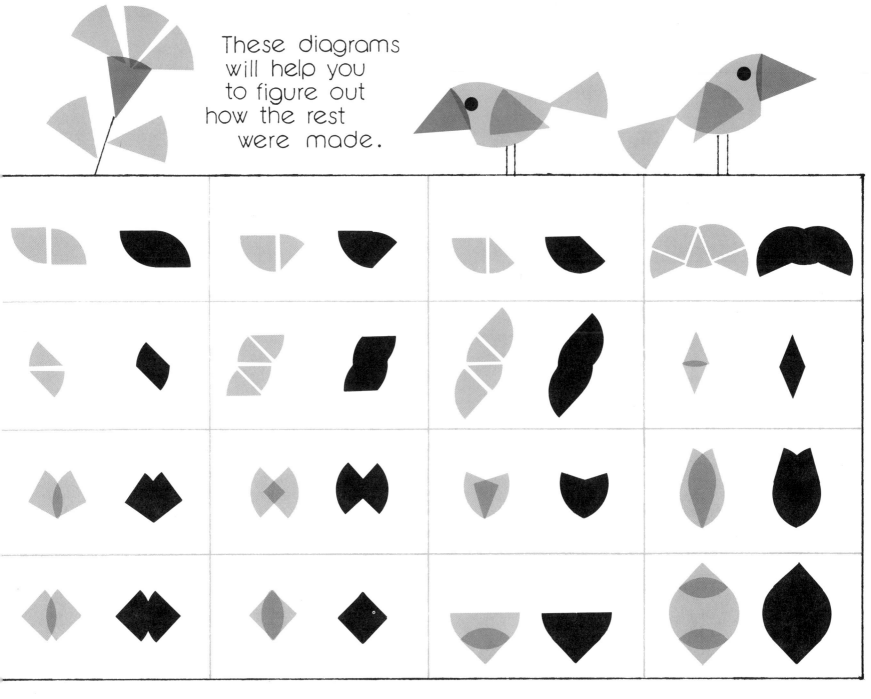

These diagrams
will help you
to figure out
how the rest
were made.

the birds

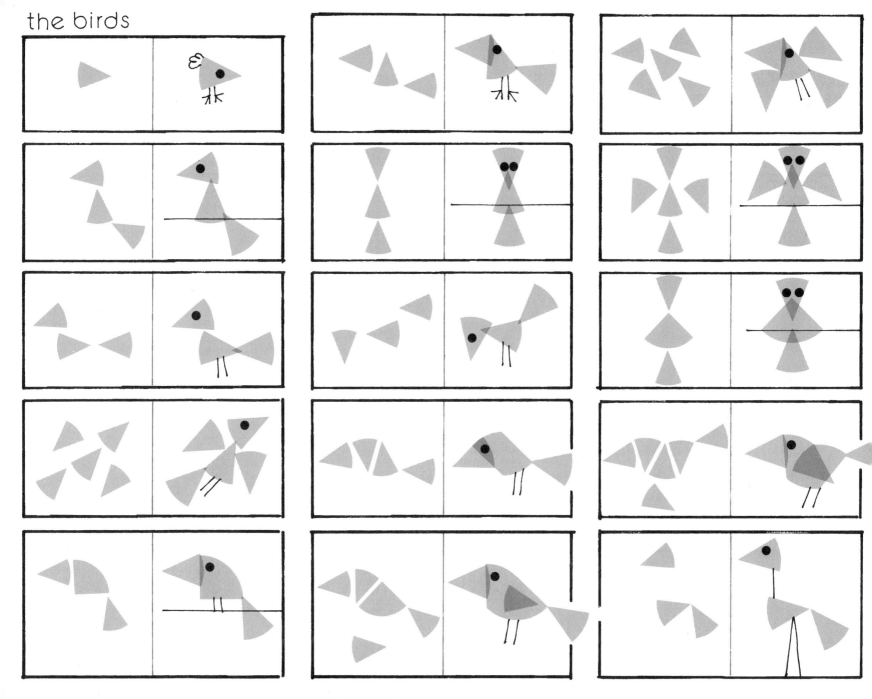

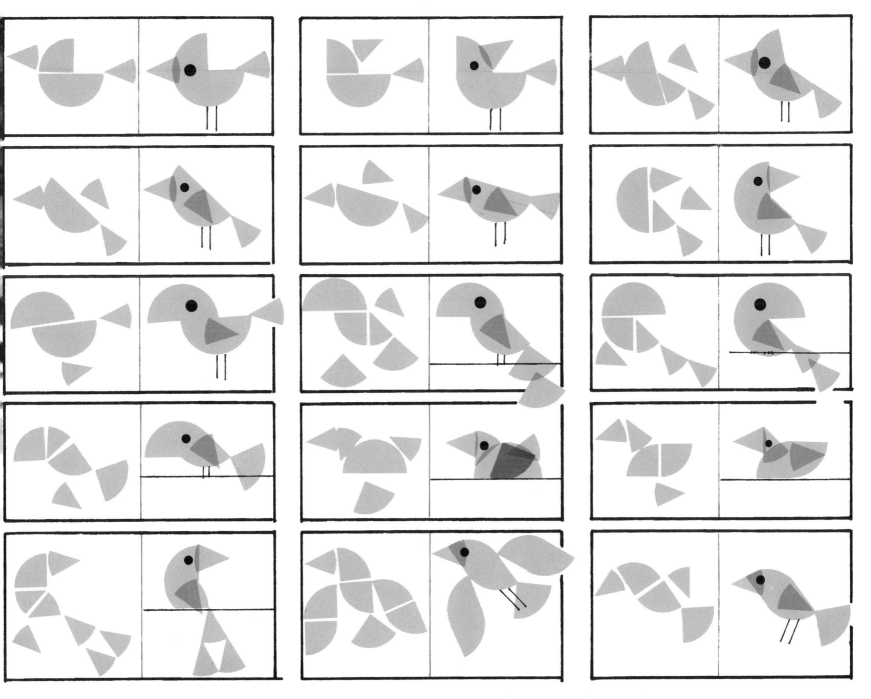

the insects

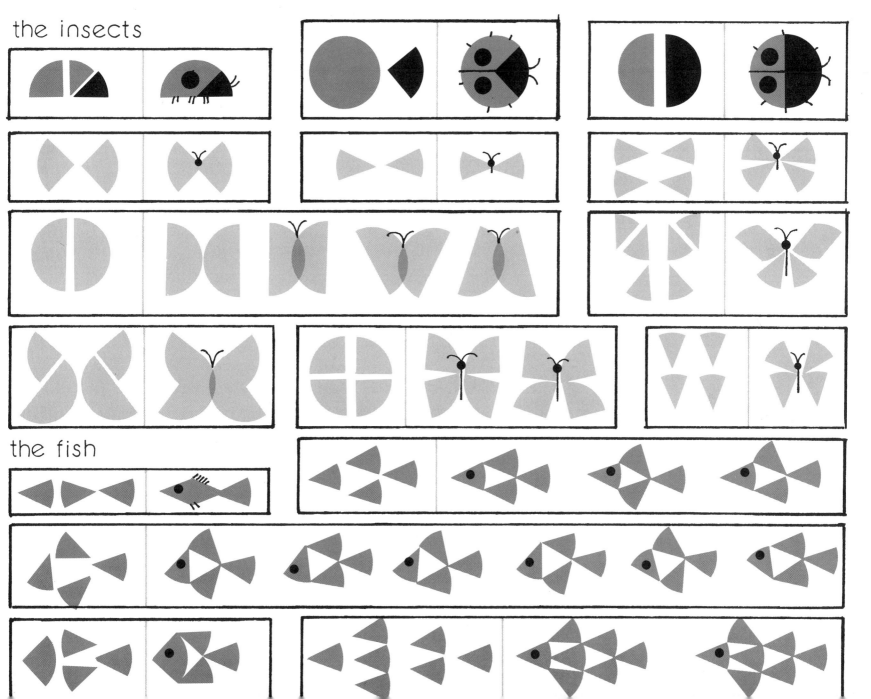

the fish

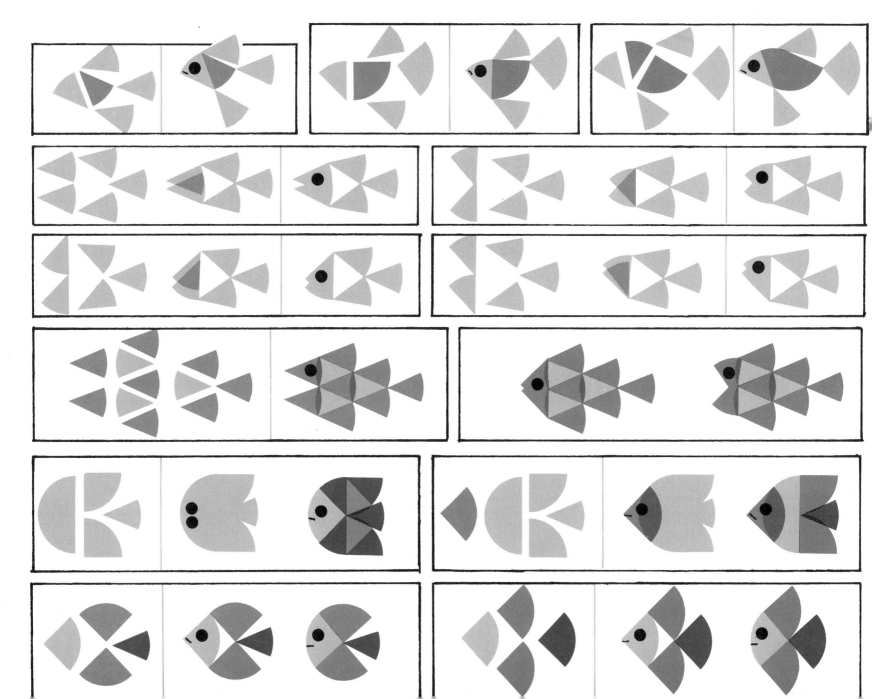

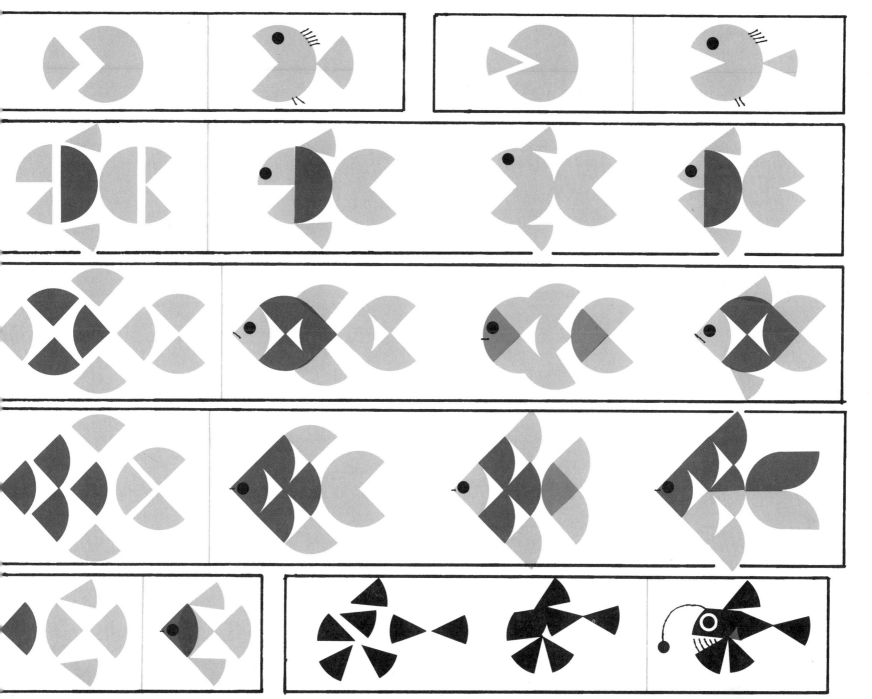

the plants

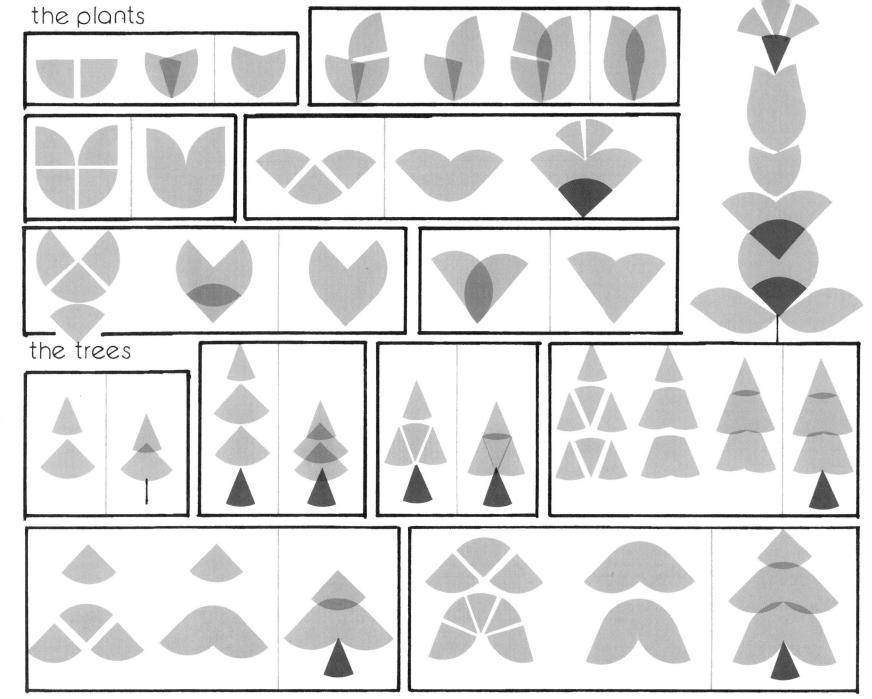

the trees

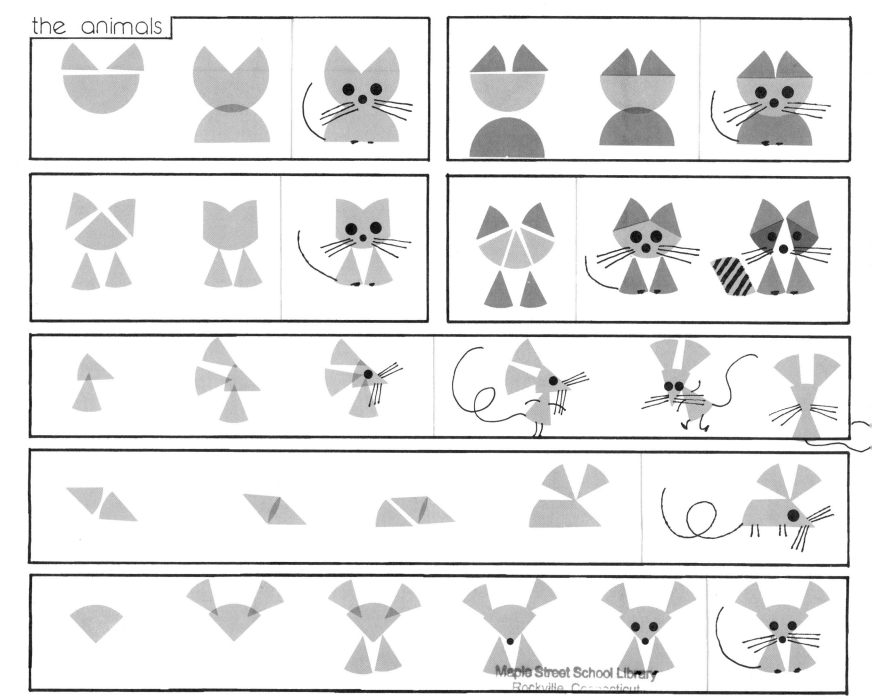

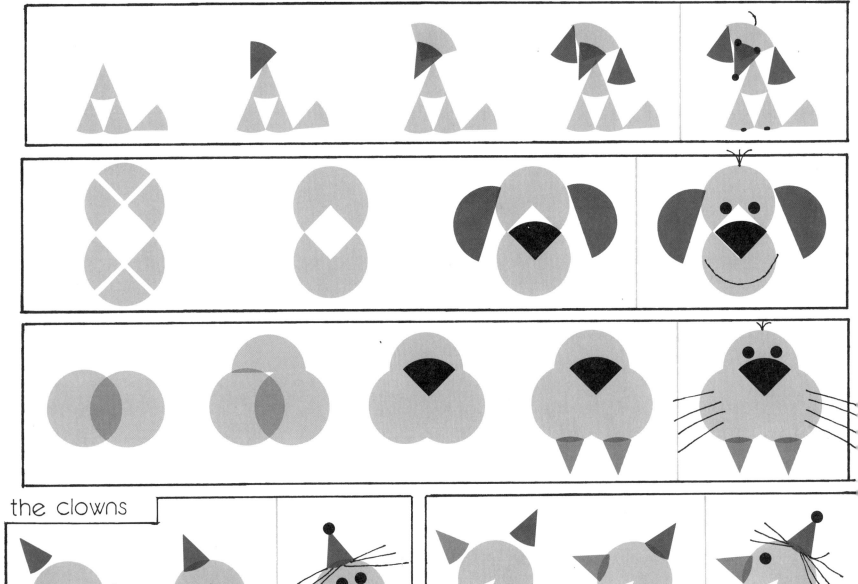

the clowns

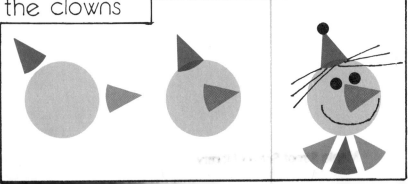

three tricky ones

Ed Emberley "drew" the pictures for this book.

Barbara and Michael Emberley prepared the

300 overlays needed to print those pictures.

Rebecca Emberley "set" the type.